The
Fireside
Cookbook

A *Between Friends* ® COOKBOOK

by
Pam McKee
Lin Webber
Ann Krum

Text by Ann Krum
Editing by Beverly J. DeWitt
Typesetting and Copy Design by Dennis Shirk

ISBN# 1-56523-041-8

A Between Friends® Cookbook
Fox Chapel Publishing Company, Inc.
Box 7948
Lancaster, PA 17604-7948
USA

Manufactured in Hong Kong

Because they always eat the meals we serve
and thank us graciously, we dedicate this book
to our husbands.

Bruce Krum
Michael McKee
Robert Webber

Table of Contents

Introduction

Dinner parties can be a lot of fun, but they can also mean plenty of work for the hostess or host. A fireside dinner can be a bit less formal and involved than an elegant soiree in the dining room. Keep things simple by selecting as many do-ahead dishes as possible. After all, the point of entertaining is to spend time with friends.

This little book offers four fireside-dinner menus (Colonial, Harvest, Snowstorm, and New Year's Eve) with recipes for all the dishes. Try all four just as they are—or follow your inspiration and substitute a favorite dish or two.

When Thomas Jefferson returned from Italy, he brought back a pasta maker and was the first to serve pasta at a colonial dinner party.

Jefferson invented the lazy Susan and the dumb waiter to minimize the intrusion of the servants. He was even known to pour the wine himself.

Martha Washington cooked at least one ham every day of the year because she never knew who or how many would be there for dinner.

Thomas Jefferson raised and enjoyed tomatoes long before others stopped believing they were poisonous.

Pity the poor soul who eats only to sustain life.

Of little fires
And gentle souls delight.
Come sit awhile
And dine with me tonight.

Anonymous

Eat slowly; only men in rags
And gluttens old in sin
Mistake themselves for carpet-bags
And tumble victuals in.

Sir Walter Raleigh

A man seldom thinks with more earnestness of anything than
he does of his supper.

Samuel Johnson

Heavenly Father, bless us,
And keep us all alive,
There's ten of us to dinner
And not enough for five.

Hodge's Grace

A poem

After a good dinner, one can forgive anyone, even one's
own relations.
Oscar Wilde

It isn't so much what's on the table that matters, as what's
on the chairs.
W.S. Gilbert

Sit down and feed, and welcome to our table.
Shakespeare, As You Like It

You tell me whar a man gits his cornpone, en I'll tell you
what his 'pinions is.
Mark Twain

Better is a dinner of herbs where love is, than a stalled ox
and hatred therewith.
Proverbs 15:17

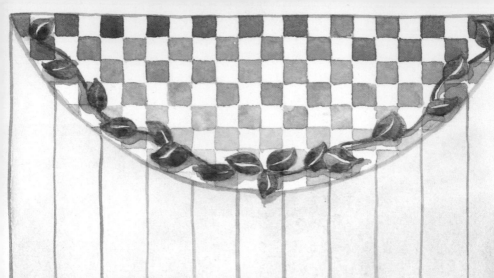

Strange to see how a good dinner and feasting reconciles everyone.
Samuel Pepy's Diary, Nov. 9, 1665

This was a good dinner enough, to be sure, but it was not a dinner to ask
a man to.
Boswell, Life of Johnson (1763)

No place is more delightful than one's own fireside.
Cicero

I believe in the fireside. I believe in the democracy of the home. I believe
in the republicanism of the family.
Ingersoll

'Tis not the meat but 'tis the appetite makes eating a delight.
Sir John Suckling

There is no love sincerer than the love of food.
George Bernard Shaw

There can be no taste at the table without love in the kitchen.
Alan Watts

That all-softening, overpowering knell, the tocsin of the soul--the dinner
bell.
Byron

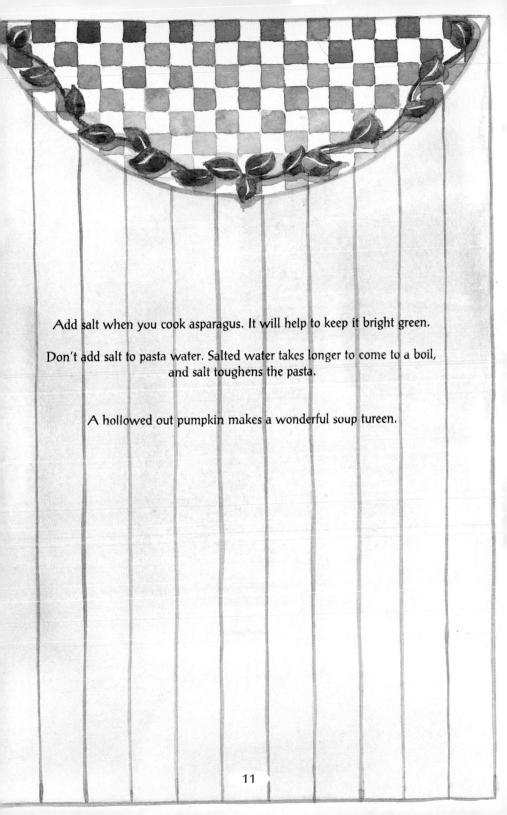

Add salt when you cook asparagus. It will help to keep it bright green.

Don't add salt to pasta water. Salted water takes longer to come to a boil, and salt toughens the pasta.

A hollowed out pumpkin makes a wonderful soup tureen.

Colonial Dinner Menu

Mushrooms on toast

Stuffed cherry tomatoes

Cream of peanut soup

Lentil casserole w/ sausage

Chicken w/ cranberries

Sally Lund

Virginia spoon bread

Gingered asparagus

Dried corn

Syllabub · Pecan pie

Apple crisp

Colonial

We lost our electricity for a day this spring and were amazed at how helpless we were. Thinking about the colonists and all the hardships they endured, I decided it would be fun to plan a colonial dinner party. To set the tone for your own party, seal the invitations with sealing wax (or substitute candle wax). Suggest that the women wear long skirts and the men their biggest and baggiest white shirts—or something else colonial.

To give this dinner authenticity, rely as little as possible on electricity. Welcome your guests with luminaries lining the front walk and porch. To make them, fill brown or white lunch bags with a couple of inches of sand and stand a candle in each one. If you feel creative, cut a design in each bag. If you have a lantern, hang it on the front porch, and place candles in the front windows.

The roaring fire in the fireplace will supply some light, but you'll also need plenty of candles. Although in the movies a single candle lights up an entire room, count on providing at least ten to illuminate your room. If you don't have enough candlesticks, make some more luminaries (cut the lunch bags to the height of the sand), stick candles in blocks of Styrofoam placed inside pewter or earthenware bowls, or use kerosene lamps. Be sure that all candles are secure in their holders and positioned where they will not accidentally be knocked over. For the finishing touch, light the powder room with candles also.

Bring out anything pewter you may have, even if it's just a single serving piece or something to put a few flowers in. Jefferson cups would be lovely for the syllabub. Set the table with ironstone china or a collection of old matched or unmatched china. (Most colonial homes probably didn't have matching china.) You might cheat a bit with the electricity and put some madrigals on the stereo.

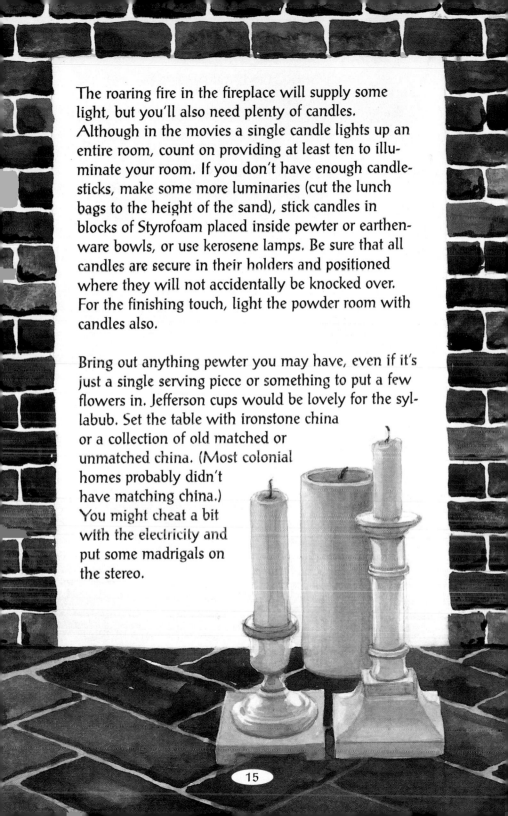

MUSHROOMS ON TOAST

I've adored mushrooms ever since my husband first cooked this dish for me. It's a great appetizer.

Melt some butter in a frying pan, add finely diced onion or shallot and as much garlic as you like, along with finely diced mushrooms, and saute. Add salt and pepper and a few splashes of white wine. Cook slowly over low heat until the liquid is reduced a bit. (You want enough liquid to soak into the toast.) Serve over toast points.

STUFFED CHERRY TOMATOES

25 cherry tomatoes
8 ounces cream cheese, softened
1 tablespoon grated onion
1 tablespoon minced parsley
Salt and pepper
1/4 cup finely diced ham or crumbled cooked bacon
Dash of Worcestershire sauce

Cut tops from tomatoes, remove pulp with a melon baller, and invert tomatoes on paper towels to drain. Combine remaining ingredients and use to stuff tomatoes.

CREAM OF PEANUT SOUP

This soup is said to have been one of George Washington's favorites.

1 quart chicken stock
2 carrots, chopped
1 yellow onion, chopped
1 cup smooth peanut butter
1 cup whipping cream or half-and-half
1/2 cup dry-roasted peanuts
Salt and pepper (to taste)
Tabasco sauce (to taste)

Place the stock in a large pot, add carrots and onion, bring to a boil, reduce heat, and simmer, covered, until vegetables are tender. Puree mixture, a little at a time, and return to pot. Stir in peanut butter and remaining ingredients, bring to a simmer, and serve.

SALLY LUNN BREAD

2 eggs, separated
1/2 cup sugar
2 cups flour, sifted after measuring
1 tablespoon baking powder
1/2 teaspoon salt
3/4 cup milk
2 tablespoons butter, melted
1/4 cup sugar

Preheat oven to 350°F. Beat egg yolks with the 1/2 cup sugar. Mix together flour, baking powder, and salt. Add dry ingredients to sugar mixture alternately with milk. Add melted butter. Beat egg whites until stiff and fold into batter. Pour into greased 9x5x3 loaf pan, sprinkle the 1/4 cup sugar on top. Bake 40 to 45 minutes.

VIRGINIA SPOON BREAD

1 cup cornmeal (white or yellow)
1 1/2 teaspoons salt
2 cups milk, scalded
2 1/2 teaspoons baking powder
2 eggs, separated

Mix cornmeal with salt and stir into the hot milk. Cook over very low heat, stirring constantly, until thick and smooth. Continue cooking for about 15 minutes, stirring now and then. Cool slightly. Stir in the baking powder and well-beaten yolks, and fold in the stiffly beaten egg whites. Turn into a greased casserole or 8" square baking pan. Bake at 375°F about 35 minutes or until firm with a brown crust.

LENTIL CASSEROLE WITH SAUSAGE

My brother and his wife sent this recipe from snowy Maine, and it seemed just right for a colonial dinner. It's a hearty and very filling main dish.

1 cup chopped onion
3/4 cup dry lentils
3/4 cup uncooked brown rice
3/4 cup shredded Cheddar cheese
2 cloves garlic, crushed
1/4 cup water
1/2 teaspoon thyme
1/2 teaspoon oregano
1/2 teaspoon basil
1/8 teaspoon sage
1/4 teaspoon salt
Freshly ground black pepper
2 cans (each 14.5 ounces) low-sodium chicken broth
1 to 2 pounds cooked hot or sweet Italian sausage, bratwurst, or your favorite sausage

Coat a 1 1/2-quart casserole with cooking spray. In it, combine all ingredients except broth. Stir. Pour broth over and stir again. Cover and bake at 350°F for 1 1/2 hours.

This recipe can be made into a side-dish by omitting the sausage.

Note: I like to add some hot pepper flakes or a little hot pepper sauce to this casserole while assembling it. If you prefer your casseroles on the moist side, you may also wish to increase the amount of broth or water.

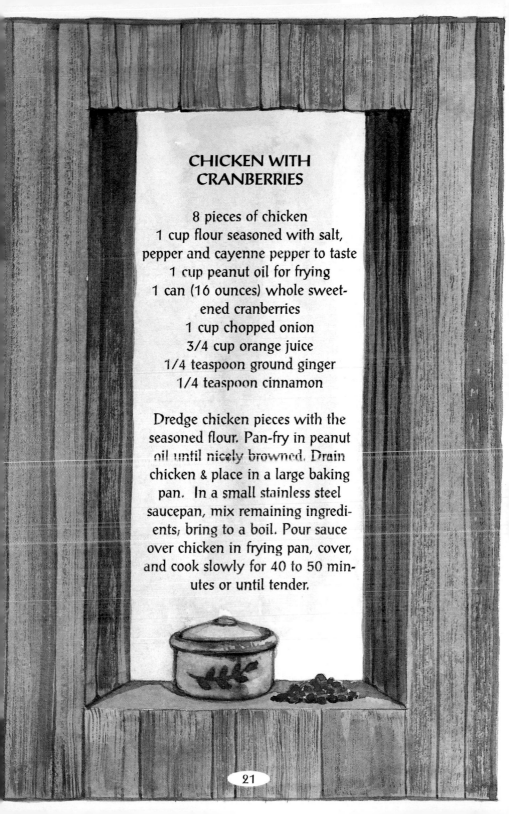

CHICKEN WITH CRANBERRIES

8 pieces of chicken
1 cup flour seasoned with salt,
pepper and cayenne pepper to taste
1 cup peanut oil for frying
1 can (16 ounces) whole sweet-
ened cranberries
1 cup chopped onion
3/4 cup orange juice
1/4 teaspoon ground ginger
1/4 teaspoon cinnamon

Dredge chicken pieces with the
seasoned flour. Pan-fry in peanut
oil until nicely browned. Drain
chicken & place in a large baking
pan. In a small stainless steel
saucepan, mix remaining ingredients; bring to a boil. Pour sauce
over chicken in frying pan, cover,
and cook slowly for 40 to 50 minutes or until tender.

DRIED CORN

1 cup dried sweet corn (Cope's)
1 1/2 cups milk
1 1/2 teaspoons salt
2 teaspoons sugar
3/4 cup light cream
2 tablespoons butter

Place corn and milk in a quart bowl, cover, and refrigerate overnight. About 30 to 45 minutes before serving time, place soaked corn, and the milk in which it soaked, salt, sugar, and light cream in a heavy 2-quart saucepan. Bring to a boil, reduce heat to low, and simmer about 30 minutes. Pour into a heated serving dish and top with butter.
Serves 4 to 6.

GINGERED ASPARAGUS

Sauté some freshly grated ginger in a little oil. When the ginger releases its juices, add asparagus, turning to coat with the ginger oil. Add a pinch of salt and a tablespoon of orange juice concentrate. Turn down the heat; add freshly ground black pepper and a little Oriental sesame oil. Cover and cook until done to your liking.

Note: Quantities are not critical with recipes of this sort. Use as much ginger as you like.

MOM'S PECAN PIE

What—other than lemon chess or sweet potatoes—could be more colonial than pecan pie? My mother's recipe is so good that it's spoiled me for any other version.

2 eggs, beaten
1 cup dark corn syrup
1/8 teaspoon salt
1/2 teaspoon vanilla
2/3 cup sugar
1/3 cup butter, melted
1 cup pecan halves

Mix all ingredients and pour into an uncooked pie shell. Bake at 350°F for 50 to 60 minutes or until filling is just set.

SYLLABUB

There are as many recipes as there are spellings for syllabub, which can be either a drink or a dessert. Probably of English origin, it has been very popular since pre-Elizabethan times, and the colonists were quite fond of it in either form.

1 cup sweet sherry
1 cup Madeira
2 lemons
4 cups heavy cream
1 teaspoon ground mace (optional)
1/2 cup sugar

Mix sherry and Madeira. Add juice from lemons. Peel outer rind of lemons and add peel to wine. Allow to stand for half an hour and then strain wine and add strained wine to heavy cream along with the mace and sugar. Beat ingredients with a rotary egg beater or electric mixer until frothy. Spoon into your most elegant glass dessert dishes or goblets and serve. Makes 12 servings.

APPLE CRISP

4 large apples, peeled and sliced
(Granny Smith apples are good)
Nutmeg and cinnamon (to taste)
1 cup sugar
1/4 cup water
1/2 cup margarine
1 cup flour, sifted after measuring

Preheat oven to 350°F. Sprinkle apples
with nutmeg, cinnamon, and 1/2 cup of
the sugar. Add water. Place in a 9"
square baking dish. Cut margarine into
remaining 1/2 cup sugar, add flour, and
mix well. Sprinkle mixture over apples
and bake 30 to 45 minutes or until
apples are of desired tenderness. Serves 6.

Notes: Some people enjoy this crisp either hot
or cold, topped with vanilla ice cream. My
family likes it best very cold, served in a bowl
with milk. We eat it for breakfast as well as
for dessert.

Harvest Dinner Menu

Mulled cider
Curried nuts
Pork chops in sour cream
Chicken Dijon
Alice's potato casserole
Sweet potato autumn
Baked tomatoes
Angel gingerbread
Lemon sauce
Cranberry ice

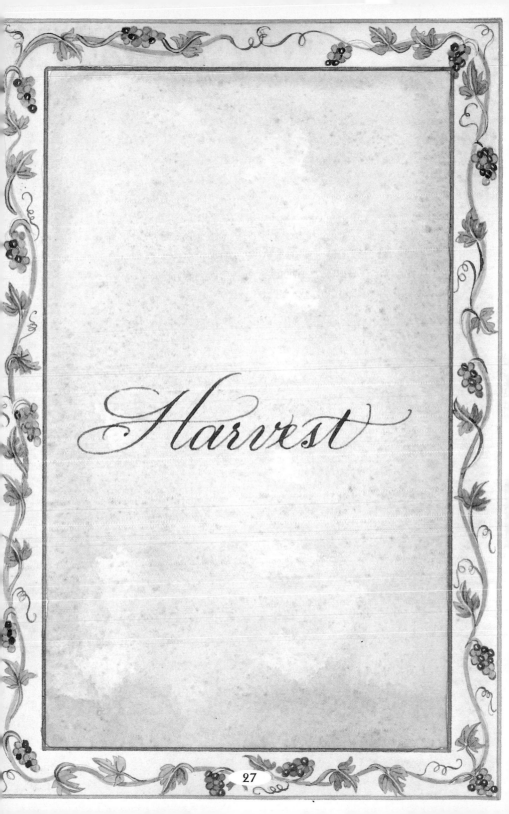

Harvest

When the long, hot days of summer pass and are replaced by the shorter, crisper ones of fall, there's a new energy and anticipation in the air. It's the perfect time for a fireside harvest supper. Make it an informal gathering where guests wear jeans and flannel shirts. After all, the more formal Thanksgiving and Christmas festivities are fast approaching.

Lots of late-blooming mums arranged in a crock make a pretty centerpiece. Or arrange branches of gold, red, orange, and yellow leaves in a copper bowl or lay them flat on the table and place shiny red and green apples on them. A pumpkin and some gourds on the hearth or mantle with leaves and brass candlesticks add to the harvest tone.

BETSY KELLY'S MULLED CIDER

Years ago, we three were in a craft cooperative, and when we had an open house or party at the shop, we always served Betsy Kelly's mulled cider. Served hot or cold, this cider drink is always a hit.

1 gallon cider
1/2 cup orange juice
1/2 cup lemon juice
1/4 cup brown sugar
1/4 cup maple syrup
Rum or rum extract to your taste
6 whole cloves
1 cinnamon stick

Combine all ingredients and heat over very low heat to dissolve sugar. Raise to a comfortable drinking temperature. Never boil or it will separate. May also be served cold. A crock pot set on its lowest setting is perfect for keeping this the right temperature.

CURRIED NUTS

Place peanuts, almonds, walnuts, or a mixture in a frying pan over fairly high heat. Keep the nuts moving in the pan. When you hear them start to pop and see them begin to brown, sprinkle a little Oriental sesame oil and curry powder on them and toss well. Salt lightly if desired.

PORK CHOPS IN SOUR CREAM

8 center-cut pork chops
1/4 cup flour
8 whole cloves
2 tablespoons butter
1 cup water
1 bay leaf
1/4 cup vinegar
2 tablespoons sugar
1 cup sour cream
Salt and pepper (to taste)

Preheat oven to 350°F. Coat chops with flour and insert a clove in each chop. Heat butter in a casserole and brown chops on both sides. Combine sour cream and remaining ingredients and pour over chops. Cover casserole and bake 1 hour.

CHICKEN DIJON

8 chicken breast halves, skinned and boned
3 tablespoons margarine
2 tablespoons flour
1 cup chicken broth
1/2 cup light cream
2 tablespoons Dijon mustard
Tomato wedges and parsley

In a large skillet, sauté chicken in margarine about 20 minutes; remove breasts. Stir flour into pan juices; add chicken broth and cream. Cook, stirring, until thick. Stir in mustard. Add chicken and heat 10 minutes. Garnish with tomato and parsley before serving.

BAKED TOMATOES

5 tomatoes
1/2 cup bread crumbs
2 tablespoons butter, melted
Chopped parsley
1 teaspoon basil
Salt (to taste)
Sesame seeds

Core tomatoes and cut in half horizontally. Mix remaining ingredients (except sesame seeds) and spread on tomato halves. Sprinkle with sesame seeds. Bake at 350°F for 15 minutes.

ALICE'S POTATO CASSEROLE

My old college friend made my preparation for
Christmas dinner a little easier with this next
recipe. Instead of mashing potatoes at the last
minute, I prepare this casserole a day or two
ahead of time. Bring it to room temperature and
heat at 350°F for 30 to 45 minutes.
Thanks Alice.

5 pounds (about 9 large) potatoes
2 packages (each 3 ounces) cream cheese
1 cup sour cream
2 teaspoons onion salt
2 tablespoons butter

Cook, drain, and mash the potatoes. Add cream
cheese, sour cream, and onion salt; beat until
fluffy. Place potatoes in a greased casserole and
dot with butter before serving.

Note: To make these potatoes a little different,
add equal parts horseradish, grainy mustard, and
chopped parsley. Don't be afraid to add a lot.

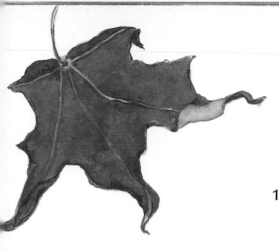

SWEET POTATOES
AUTUMN

3 cups mashed cooked sweet
potatoes
1 cup sugar
1/2 teaspoon salt
2 eggs, well beaten
1/4 cup (1/2 stick) butter, melted
1/2 cup milk
1 tablespoon vanilla extract
1/2 teaspoon ground nutmeg
1/2 teaspoon cinnamon

Topping:
1 cup brown sugar
1/2 cup flour
1 cup chopped pecans
1/4 cup (1/2 stick) butter

Mix all ingredients except those for topping and place in an ovenproof casserole. Combine topping ingredients and spread over potatoes. Bake, uncovered, for 30 minutes at 350° F.

PETE'S ANGEL GINGERBREAD

My brother used to eat slabs of this gingerbread slathered with butter. Some people prefer whipped cream with it, but I think butter enhances the flavor. It's also wonderful with Lemon Sauce (recipe on page 38).

1/2 cup shortening
1 cup sugar
2 eggs
1/2 cup molasses
2 1/3 cups flour
1/2 teaspoon salt
1 teaspoon baking soda
1 teaspoon ground ginger (or more if you love ginger)
1/4 teaspoon ground nutmeg
1/4 teaspoon cinnamon
1/4 teaspoon ground allspice
1 cup hot water

Cream shortening and sugar. Add eggs and molasses. Beat well. Sift together dry ingredients and add alternately with hot water. Pour batter into a 9" x 13" greased and floured pan and bake at 350°F for 45 minutes.

CRANBERRY ICE

1 quart cranberries
2 cups water
2 cups sugar
1/4 cup lemon juice
1 teaspoon grated orange zest or 1/2 cup orange juice
2 cups cold water (part raspberry juice may be used)

In a heavy saucepan, cook cranberries with 2 cups water and
sugar for about 10 minutes or until skins pop. Rub through a
fine sieve or puree in a food processor to make a smooth pulp.
Stir in remaining ingredients. Pour into refrigerator trays and
freeze until firm, stirring 2 or 3 times during the freezing process.
Serves 8.

LEMON SAUCE

1/2 cup sugar
1 tablespoon cornstarch
1 cup boiling water
1 tablespoon butter
1 tablespoon lemon juice
1 tablespoon grated lemon zest

In a small, heavy saucepan, thoroughly mix sugar, cornstarch,
and water. Bring to a boil, stirring constantly, and boil 1 minute.
Remove from heat. Stir in remaining ingredients.
Keep hot until time to serve.

Snowstorm Dinner Menu

Mexican chocolate olé
Sausage starters
Roasted garlic
Bruis chili
Shrimp scampi & pasta
Welsh rabbit
Spinach salad
Dressing #1
Dressing #2
Creamy blue cheese dressing
Cracker pudding
Gam's custard

Snowstorm

The next time snow is predicted, call a few friends and arrange a skating or sledding party. Invite everyone back to your house afterward for a relaxed, casual dinner.

Lay a fire before you go out so that it will be ready to light the minute you return. Set up whatever tables you'll need and cover them with old quilts or army blankets—anything that looks warm and cozy. Or use winter scarves folded to the size of placemats or one long scarf as a table runner. Place pinecones and red candles on the tables. If you have an old sled that didn't go along for the ride, use it in place of a coffee table for the appetizers. Run a heavy cord across the mantle with plenty of clothespins so that everyone can hang their gloves and mittens to dry. Have a record, tape, or CD of George Winston's Winter ready to go.

MEXICAN CHOCOLATE OLE

1 quart milk
5 ounces semi-sweet chocolate
3 cinnamon sticks
1 teaspoon vanilla

In a saucepan combine milk, chocolate, and cinnamon sticks. Cook, stirring, over low heat until chocolate melts. Remove from heat and add vanilla. Remove cinnamon sticks and beat rapidly with an egg beater to incorporate lots of air, until mixture is nice and foamy. Serve in warm mugs.

ITALIAN SAUSAGE STARTERS

Bake two to three pounds of sausage (hot, sweet, or both) for 1 hour at 350°F. Cut into bite-sized pieces and mix with a jar of any good commercial pepper salad—one full of hot peppers, onions, and other enticing flavors. Serve hot.

ROASTED GARLIC

Don't peel the garlic heads; simply cut off the top 1/4 to 1/2 inch. Place heads in a small baking dish and drizzle 1 tablespoon of olive oil over each head. Cover and bake at 350°F for 1 hour.

Note: Sprinkle with salt, pepper, and grated Parmesan cheese halfway through baking time if desired. The garlic becomes soft and mild and may be spread on crackers or toasted bread. A little soft cheese is a good accompaniment, too.

BRU'S CHILI

Bruce's chili will warm you even on the coldest day.

1 pound dry pinto beans
1 pound ground beef
1 large onion, diced
Salt and ground black pepper (to taste)
1 small can (6 ounces) tomato paste
1 can (16 ounces) stewed tomatoes
1 teaspoon cayenne pepper
2 diced red chili peppers (remove seeds; wash hands after handling)
2 teaspoons chili powder
1 tablespoon Worcestershire sauce
1 teaspoon cumin
Dash hot pepper flakes

Cover pinto beans with several inches of water; soak overnight. Drain beans, add fresh water to cover, bring to a boil, reduce heat, and simmer 1 hour. Drain.

Brown ground beef and onion; pour off any grease; season with salt and pepper. Combine all ingredients in a large crockpot, mixing thoroughly. Cook at least 5 hours on low, or until beans are of desired tenderness. Adjust seasonings before serving.

SPINACH SALAD

Wash, tear, and dry spinach leaves; place in a bowl. Top with thinly sliced hard-cooked eggs, crumbled bacon, and lots of thinly sliced red onion. Serve with one or a choice of the following dressings.

ZESTY SPINACH SALAD DRESSING

1 cup salad oil
3/4 cup sugar
1/3 cup ketchup
1/4 cup vinegar (balsamic if available)
1 tablespoon Worcestershire sauce
1/2 teaspoon salt
1 medium onion, sliced

Puree all ingredients in blender. Refrigerate.

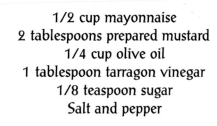

1/2 cup mayonnaise
2 tablespoons prepared mustard
1/4 cup olive oil
1 tablespoon tarragon vinegar
1/8 teaspoon sugar
Salt and pepper

Combine all ingredients
well. Refrigerate.

CREAMY BLUE CHEESE DRESSING

1/4 pound blue or Roquefort cheese
3 tablespoons light cream
1/2 cup mayonnaise
1/4 cup wine vinegar
1/8 teaspoon salt
1/8 teaspoon pepper
1 teaspoon prepared mustard
6 tablespoons salad oil

Mash cheese with cream until
smooth. Add remaining ingredients
and beat until creamy.
Refrigerate. Makes 1 cup.

SHRIMP SCAMPI AND PASTA

1 3/4 cups defatted chicken broth
2 tablespoons chopped garlic
1/4 cup chopped shallots
1/4 cup chopped parsley
1/2 pound pasta (angel hair, vermicelli, or linguini)
1 pound peeled raw shrimp
Freshly ground black pepper

Put a large pot of water on to boil for the pasta. In a large saucepan, combine broth, garlic, and 3 tablespoons each of the shallots and parsley. Bring to a simmer and cook about 2 minutes.

Add pasta to boiling water and cook according to package directions. Add shrimp to broth, stir well, and cook 3 minutes or until shrimp turn pink. Add remaining 1 tablespoon shallots.

Drain pasta and place on individual serving plates. Using a slotted spoon, arrange shrimp on pasta, ladle broth over shrimp. Sprinkle with pepper and remaining 1 tablespoon parsley. Serves 4 as a main dish.

WELSH RABBIT

1 cup milk
1 pound sharp Cheddar cheese, grated
2 teaspoons dried mustard
2 teaspoons Worcestershire sauce
2 well-beaten eggs

Heat milk over very low heat; add cheese and cook, stirring constantly, until cheese melts. Add seasonings and eggs to which a small amount of hot milk and cheese mixture has been added to prevent curdling of eggs and continue to cook, stirring, until mixture thickens and is creamy.

Note: When I was a child, this was always served over Saltine crackers and topped with bacon. Try it over toast triangles, split corn bread, or English muffins. The rabbit cools quickly, making this a good chafing dish meal, or reheat it quickly in the microwave.

CRACKER PUDDING

This recipe comes from Groff's Farm Restaurant in Mt. Joy, Pennsylvania, where it's served before dinner. The proprietress believes that guests may be too full for dessert after eating all that is offered there. Since we eat lighter at our house, we have it for dessert. If you don't care for coconut, try this anyway. I can't stand coconut, but love cracker pudding.

2 eggs, separated
1 quart milk
2/3 cup sugar
2 cups broken (not rolled into crumbs) Saltine crackers
1 cup grated coconut
1 teaspoon vanilla

Beat egg whites until stiff and set aside. In a heavy 3-quart pot or Dutch oven, heat milk almost to the boiling point. In a bowl, beat the egg yolks and sugar until frothy and light. Gradually add to the hot milk. Reduce heat to medium. Place the crackers and coconut in the milk mixture and stir constantly until the pudding bubbles thickly like oatmeal. Remove from heat and add vanilla. Fold in the thickly beaten egg whites. Serve warm or cold.

Note: For a fancier presentation, top pudding with meringue and bake until golden.

GAM'S CUSTARD

3 cups milk
1/3 cup sugar
3 eggs
1 teaspoon vanilla

Whip all ingredients together, divide among 7 or 8 custard cups. Place cups in baking pan and pour water around them to a depth of about 1 inch. Bake at 350°F for 1 hour.

New Year's Eve Dinner

Marinated water chestnuts

Crab dip

Chick pea nuts

Curry with accompaniments

Shrimp creole

Barbecued chicken

Tammy's rice

Lemoned green beans

Chocolate pound cake

Hot fudge sauce

Lemon sponge

New Year's Eve

Many people expect New Year's Eve to be full of hoopla, confetti, a thousand balloons falling from the ceiling, love with the perfect stranger, and sequined dresses. After all, that's the way it is in the movies. With such high expectations, it's no wonder that the holiday often falls short.

Several years ago we began a New Year's Eve tradition of our own. We get together with four other couples for a fireside New Year's Eve dinner—one that's more festive and elegant than our usual gatherings. Everyone dresses up, and a few of the men even wear tuxedos.

The first year we had a "Mystery Night." Another year the host took photographs of each couple, his daughter made pencil drawings from them, and we all received a really special portrait. A third year we divided into teams and took an "Arctic Survival Test." Other times we just visit or play word games, but each year it's a gathering of ten people who are extremely comfortable together and whose only expectations are to welcome the New Year among best friends.

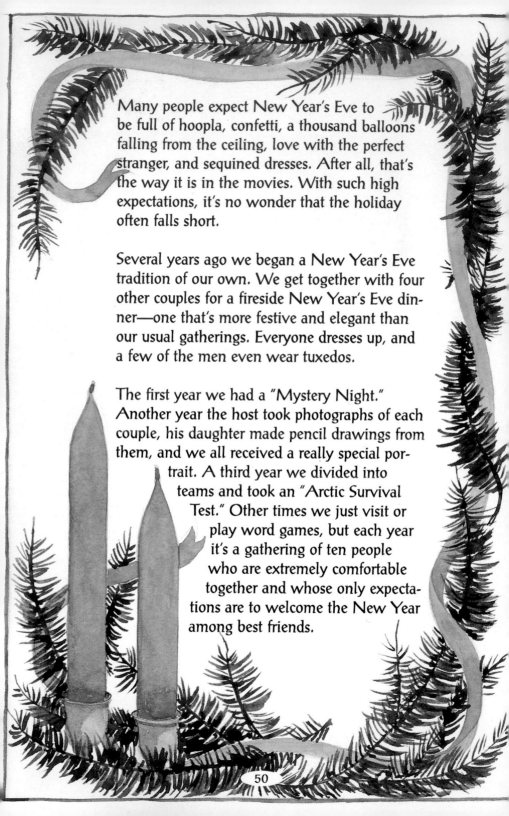

There's no
need to deco-
rate—all your holidays things
should still be displayed. A
few new long white candles
and maybe a rejuvenation
of your greens, and you're
ready to go. For ten people, a
buffet is in order. Provide good
seating arrangements for fireside
dining, especially if you're going
formal. Balancing food on your
lap detracts from the elegance of the
occasion. Be sure each chair has a cock-
tail or other small table beside it. If
you have space, set up the buffet table
in the room in which you'll be dining. Dress it with your prettiest white
damask tablecloth. Place a low bowl
of greens on it and weave a shiny ribbon
through them. Use more of the same ribbon to tie the napkins and silverware
into little bundles before placing them in
a basket.

Now's a good time to get out everything silver you own, give
each piece its semiannual polish (if you haven't already done that
for the holidays), and use it everywhere. Adorn the mantle with
an array of candlesticks (matched or unmatched) set on a bed of
greens and sporting elegant tapers. Weave a ribbon that matches
the one on the buffet table through the greenery on the mantle,
letting it trail down both sides.

MARINATED WATER CHESTNUTS

2 cans (each 5 ounces) water chestnuts
1/4 cup soy sauce
2 tablespoons sugar
1 pound bacon

Marinate water chestnuts in mixture of soy sauce and sugar for 1/2 hour. Cut bacon in half crosswise; wrap each chestnut in 1/2 slice bacon, securing with at toothpick. Bake at 350°F for 30 to 35 minutes, or until bacon is crisp.

BAKED CRAB DIP

8 ounces cream cheese, softened
1 tablespoon milk
6 ounces crabmeat (fresh, frozen, or canned)
2 tablespoons finely chopped onion
1/2 tablespoon horseradish
Salt and pepper
Slivered almonds

Thoroughly combine all ingredients except almonds. Place in an ovenproof dish; sprinkle top with almonds. Bake at 375°F for 15 minutes.

CHICKEN CURRY

I first served this basic curry recipe shortly after I was married. It's always been a hit, especially at parties.

3 tablespoons butter
1/4 cup minced onion
1 1/2 teaspoons curry powder (or to taste)
3 tablespoons flour
3/4 teaspoon salt
1/8 teaspoon ground ginger
1 cup chicken broth
1 cup milk
2 cups cut-up cooked chicken
1/2 teaspoon lemon juice

Over low heat in a heavy saucepan, melt butter. Add onion and curry powder and saute, blend in flour and seasonings. Cook over low heat until mixture bubbles and is smooth. Remove from heat. Stir in broth and milk. Return to heat and bring to a boil, stirring constantly. Boil 1 minute. Add chicken and lemon juice and heat. Serves 4 as a main dish.

Note: This recipe can be easily doubled or tripled. Serve over plain white rice or Tammy's Rice. Offer five or six of the following accompaniments:

Chutney
Tomato wedges
Chopped salted peanuts
Slivered salted almonds
Chopped onion
Chopped hard-cooked eggs
Crumbled bacon
Sweet or sour pickles
Pineapple chunks
Sliced avocado

CHICK-PEA NUTS

1 can (20 ounces) chick-peas (garbanzo beans)
1/4 teaspoon garlic powder
1/2 teaspoon onion powder
Cayenne pepper (to taste)

Drain chick-peas, combine seasonings and sprinkle over chick-peas, stirring to distribute. Spread on nonstick cookie sheet and bake at 350°F for 40 minutes, stirring now and then to encourage even cooking and prevent sticking. Makes 2 cups.

TAMMY'S RICE

3 tablespoons butter
2 onions, chopped
2 tablespoons Worcestershire sauce
1 cup white rice
2 cans (each 14.5 ounces) beef consomme

In a skillet, melt butter, add onions and saute until soft and translucent. Add Worcestershire sauce. Put mixture in casserole dish along with rice and consomme, stir. Bake covered at 350°F for 1 hour.

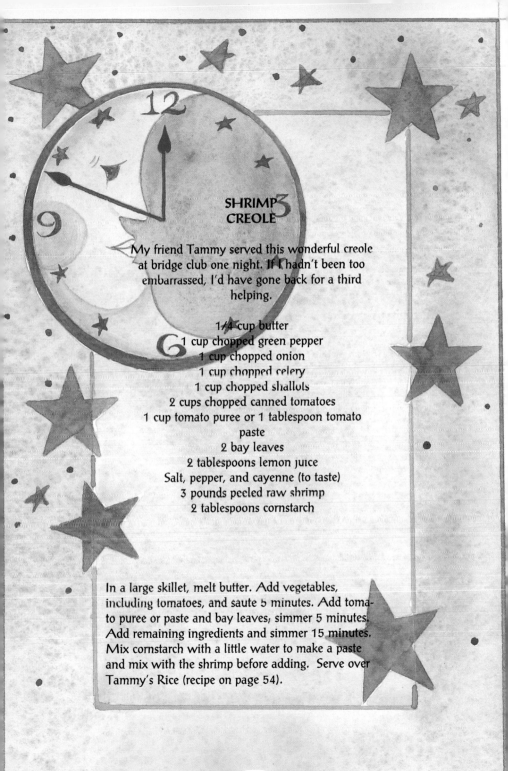

SHRIMP CREOLE

My friend Tammy served this wonderful creole at bridge club one night. If I hadn't been too embarrassed, I'd have gone back for a third helping.

1/4 cup butter
1 cup chopped green pepper
1 cup chopped onion
1 cup chopped celery
1 cup chopped shallots
2 cups chopped canned tomatoes
1 cup tomato puree or 1 tablespoon tomato paste
2 bay leaves
2 tablespoons lemon juice
Salt, pepper, and cayenne (to taste)
3 pounds peeled raw shrimp
2 tablespoons cornstarch

In a large skillet, melt butter. Add vegetables, including tomatoes, and saute 5 minutes. Add tomato puree or paste and bay leaves, simmer 5 minutes. Add remaining ingredients and simmer 15 minutes. Mix cornstarch with a little water to make a paste and mix with the shrimp before adding. Serve over Tammy's Rice (recipe on page 54).

BARBECUED CHICKEN

8 chicken pieces
Salt and pepper
One sliced medium onion

Barbecue Sauce
2 tablespoons vinegar
2 tablespoons Worcestershire sauce
1 teaspoon paprika
1 teaspoon chili powder
3/4 cup catsup
3/4 water

Preheat oven to 300°F. Place chicken in a 13" x 9" baking dish; sprinkle with salt and pepper; top with onion. Combine all sauce ingredients and pour over chicken; cover tightly with aluminum foil. Bake 2 hours, removing foil during the final 15 minutes to brown chicken. Serve over Tammy's Rice (recipe on page 54).

LEMONED GREEN BEANS

Cook fresh green beans until tender in a large amount of boiling salted water. Drain. Pour Lemon Butter (see below) over beans, add coarse black pepper and a little salt, and toss to coat.

LEMON BUTTER

Melt 1 or 2 tablespoons butter. Mix 1/2 teaspoon cornstarch with 2 tablespoons water; add to butter along with 1 teaspoon lemon juice. Cook, stirring, until smooth and clear.

LEMON SPONGE

This recipe of my mother-in-law's is a favorite at our house.
These custards are delicious and make a fine light dessert
for a heavy meal.

1 1/2 cups sugar
2 tablespoons flour
3 eggs, separated
Juice and grated zest of 1 lemon (more if you love lemon)
1 tablespoon melted butter
1 cup milk

Combine sugar and flour; mix in egg yolks. Add lemon juice and zest, butter, and milk. Mix well. Beat egg whites until fluffy; fold into lemon mixture. Divide mixture evenly among 7 or 8 custard cups. Set cups in a baking pan; place pan in oven and pour water around cups to a depth of about 1 inch. Bake at 350°F for 30 to 35 minutes, until the tops puff up and turn golden. Remove custard cups from baking pan and cool on wire rack (the tops will fall); refrigerate.

Janice Brenner's Mother's Chocolate Cake

Janice Breener, a college friend, would often receive this pound cake from her mother. We would descend like locusts on poor Janice's room and devour every crumb of this wonderful cake.

1 1/2 cups (3 sticks) margarine
5 cups sugar
5 eggs
3 cups sifted flour
1/2 teaspoon baking powder
1/2 teaspoon salt
1/2 cup unsweetened cocoa
1 cup milk
2 teaspoons vanilla extract

Cream margarine and sugar. Add eggs, one at a time, mixing after each addition. Sift together dry ingredients. Add alternately to creamed mixture with the milk to which the vanilla has been added. Mix well. Pour into greased and floured 10 inch tube pan or angel food cake pan. Bake at 325°F for 1 hour 20 minutes.

Note: I generally just sprinkle this cake with powdered sugar when it has cooled. Real dessert fanciers like it with vanilla ice cream and Hot Fudge Sauce (recipe on page 59).

Hot Fudge Sauce

1/2 cup evaporated milk
2 squares unsweetened chocolate
3/4 cup sugar
3 tablespoons butter
Dash salt
3/4 teaspoon vanilla extract

In the top of a double boiler, slowly heat milk and chocolate until chocolate melts. Add sugar, butter, and salt, cooking and stirring over medium-low heat until sauce is smooth. Keep warm until serving time, or if made ahead, refrigerate and reheat before serving.

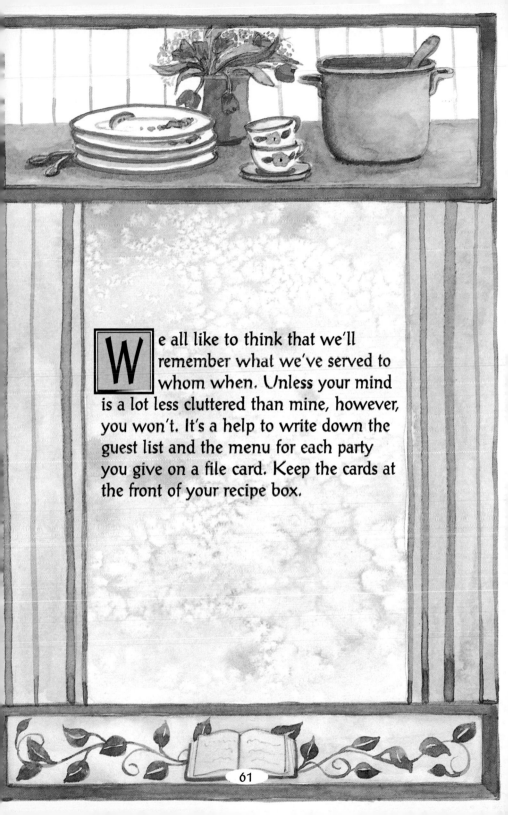

We all like to think that we'll remember what we've served to whom when. Unless your mind is a lot less cluttered than mine, however, you won't. It's a help to write down the guest list and the menu for each party you give on a file card. Keep the cards at the front of your recipe box.

INDEX

INDEX

Between Friends®
COOKBOOK SERIES

Titles Currently Available:

Afternoon Teas
The ultimate teas gift book! Browse through these beautiful pages while reading about the history of teas and the tea ceremony - then plan your own special event.
Recipes from simple to elegant, yet practical for today's cook. A variety of suggested menus are presented with all recipes included inside. This finely-appointed book is sure to become a favorite.

Afternoon Teas
ISBN #1-56523-040-X
Perfectbound, 64 pages, watercolors throughout.
$7.95

The Fireside Cookbook
Look inside this book for a wonderful collection of ideas and recipes for hosting creative dinners. From romantic dining to family get-togethers, this is a delicious and fun cookbook. Includes sample menus and hints for such themed dinners as New Years Eve, Colonial Williamsburg Style, Snowstorm Dinner and more.
Exquisite watercolors shine from every page, making this book a treasure to keep or give.

Fireside Dining
ISBN #1-56523-041-8
Perfectbound, 64 pages, 5.5 x 8.5, watercolors throughout.
$7.95

*Available from all bookstores
and fine gift shops.*

If you cannot find these titles at your favorite store you may order by mail. Please send $7.95 + $1.00 postage to:

Fox Chapel Book Orders
Box 7948
Lancaster, PA 17604-7948